First published in the United Kingdom in 2011
by Ski Solutions Limited, 84 Pembroke Road,
Kensington, London W8 6NX.

www.skisolutions.com

Copyright © Ski Solutions Limited.

All rights reserved. No part of this publication may be
reproduced or transmitted in any form or by any means,
electronic or mechanical, including photocopy, recording
or any other information storage and retrieval system,
without prior permission in writing from the publisher.

ISBN 978-0-9570137-0-4

Designed by www.cubiquitymedia.com

UNPARALLELED

25 Unforgettable Ski Experiences

FOREWORD

Over the years, I have been lucky enough to travel the globe looking for exciting winter sports adventures for my role as a presenter on BBC Ski Sunday and High Altitude. I have had some truly remarkable experiences; some exhilarating, some good, some bad and some downright terrifying.

We all love a ski holiday; the scenery in the mountains is always spectacular and the excitement of skiing or snowboarding is hard to beat. So to celebrate their 25 year anniversary, Ski Solutions have designed this book to show you a host of inspiring experiences available in the world of winter sport. For instance, how would you like to tackle the world's longest black run, heli-ski for a weekend in the Aosta Valley, see, up close, some of the world's most spectacular glaciers or bathe in a Japanese hot spring with the local snow monkey population?

All the proceeds from this book will go to Make-A-Wish Foundation® UK, which also has its 25th birthday this year. Over the years, the charity has given hope and joy to thousands of children who have had to struggle with terrible hardship in their young lives. There are over 20,000 children in the UK living with life-threatening conditions. For these children just the chance to ride a horse, drive a car or meet their favourite celebrities not only gives them a wonderful experience they will never forget, but can also be a much needed release from living day to day with illness or disability. Skiing is just one of the many opportunities Make-A-Wish Foundation® UK is able to give to these children.

Every day, these children and their families show far more courage than it takes to jump out of the start hut at Kitzbühel, knowing that you are about to hurtle down the almost sheer face of the Hahnenkamm at 90mph, more courage than it took me to make a Tyrolean traverse between the two peaks of Double Cone, 1600m above Queenstown in New Zealand. Theirs is the sort of courage that enables them to face each day as it comes. These children are an inspiration to us all.

Enjoy this book, and I hope you feel inspired to embark on one of these experiences yourself.

Graham Bell

NO FRIENDS   01
ON A POWDER DAY
Vail, USA

02   A JOURNEY
TO FALL IN LOVE WITH
Swiss Alps, Switzerland

PARTY IN YOUR SKI BOOTS   03
St Anton, Austria

04   ALL BLACK AND WHITE
Alpe d' Huez, France

NOT JUST FOR HIGH FLIERS   05
Aosta Valley, Italy

06   MY FAIR LADY
Banff, Canada

SHAKEN, NOT STIRRED   07
Mürren, Switzerland

08   CALIFORNIA DREAMING
Lake Tahoe, USA

CHUKKAS AWAY   09
Klosters, Switzerland

10   PARK AND GLIDE
Rocky Mountains, Canada

SKI SUNDAY... AND MONDAY,   11
TUESDAY, WEDNESDAY...
Kitzbühel, Austria

12   MONKEY BUSINESS
Nagano, Japan

IT MUST BE LOVE   13
Aspen, USA

14   BUON APPETITO
Courmayeur, Italy

DON'T FORGET YOUR SNORKEL   15
Kicking Horse, Canada

16   LA FOLIE, C'EST JOLIE
Val d' Isère, France

VIEW FROM THE TOP TABLE   17
Zermatt, Switzerland

18   PEAK TO CREEK
Whistler, Canada

PARK LIFE   19
Laax, Switzerland

20   THE WILD, WILD WEST
Telluride, USA

SUN, SKI, SURF   21
Hawaii, USA

22   A TOUCH OF CLASS
Lech, Austria

IT'S A FAMILY AFFAIR   23
Saas Fee, Switzerland

24   SKI TO THE STARS
3 Vallées, France

CHALLENGE OF A LIFETIME   25
Courmayeur, Italy

CONTENTS

An experience is a life-changing adventure, a chance to enjoy something incredible and far removed from everyday life that you will remember forever. So Ski Solutions has joined forces with Make-A-Wish Foundation® UK to offer one of the greatest experiences available – the chance to grant the wish of a child living with a life-threatening illness.

Make-A-Wish Foundation® is a worldwide charity that in the UK alone has granted over 7,000 wishes and has been changing lives since 1986. Children with life-threatening illnesses, some with just a few weeks to live, have had flights in helicopters, swum with dolphins, and met Santa in Lapland. Make-A-Wish Foundation® UK has turned these children's wishes into a magical and memorable reality.

This year, both Make-A-Wish Foundation® UK and Ski Solutions are celebrating 25 years of creating memories that will last a lifetime, and you can share in the feel-good factor this creates by taking up one, or more, of the life-changing experiences included in this book. Not only are all of the profits from the sale of this book going to Make-A-Wish Foundation® UK, but every time you purchase one of the 25 experiences included here, or indeed any holiday from Ski Solutions, you will be given the option to round up the price to the nearest £5, with these extra pounds going directly to the charity.

If you would prefer to support us in a more active way, sign up to take part in the Ski Solutions' 'Ski the World' event, where teams of two will raise sponsorship money to attempt to ski the combined vertical of the highest mountain on each continent – over 43,000 thigh-burning metres – over a weekend in Courmayeur, Italy (see experience 25 for more details).

We hope you find enjoyment and inspiration from this book, and next time you're embarking on your own ski experience of a lifetime, please spare a thought, and some cash, to help us create magical experiences for others.

Neil Jones
Chief Executive
Make-A-Wish Foundation® UK

Craig Burton
Managing Director
Ski Solutions

Charity Registration Nos. 295672/SC037479

If you're a believer in the mantra "no friends on a powder day", you could be friendless in Vail pretty much your whole stay. With a staggering average snowfall of 8.5 metres each winter, Vail gets more than its fair share of fresh, fluffy snow over its 5,289 acres. With its endless, adventurous terrain and seven vast treeless Back Bowls to explore, you're onto a safe bet for some truly epic days.

But don't just head straight to the Back Bowls – Blue Sky Basin and Game Creek are worth a detour for their challenging tree runs and powder-filled slopes, and for a backcountry treat, head out to Minturn Mile with a guide. Once you're done making fresh tracks all over the mountain, reclaim your friends over a victory beer.

01 / NO FRIENDS ON A POWDER DAY

A JOURNEY TO
FALL IN LOVE WITH
02 \

The world-renowned ski resorts of Zermatt and St Moritz deserve to be arrived at in style. So why not book a first class ticket on the Glacier Express, the elegant train that travels between the two, bringing a touch of old-fashioned glamour to travel. After all, these are two of the most classic of ski destinations in the Alps.

The seven and a half hour journey wends its way through the Swiss Alps, taking you back to the golden era of travel, by way of the heights of the Oberalp Pass, down to the depths of the Rhine Canyon, from the timeless elegance of St Moritz to the striking beauty of Zermatt, at the foot of the Matterhorn.

Enjoy panoramic views from the train carriages of mountain lakes, steep cliffs and pristine forests. Deep ravines and bizarre rock formations pass by, broken up by gently sloping meadows and chocolate box villages.

Having left one haven of Alpine royalty at the end of the railway line, it's a joy to find another at your destination. As is always the case on the greatest trips; on the Glacier Express, the journey itself is the ultimate destination.

You'll no doubt hear the Mooserwirt before you see it. Ski round the last corner of the Blue No 1 piste approaching St Anton, and into view comes a large pine Tyrolean chalet with a packed terrace of people spilling onto the snow. Pounding Europop blares out of a sound system that wouldn't be out of place at Wembley and before you know it you'll have joined the hundreds of skiers stomping their ski boots on any available flat surface in appreciation of the DJ. This is the Mooserwirt, home to epic après-ski and, as the legend goes, more sales of beer than any other bar in the Alps.

Step inside, if you can make your way through the crowds, by 3.30pm for the official start to the party – the 'Final Countdown' blasts out, the window shutters roll down and a dazzling light show plays out across the bar. Incredibly strong waiters bustle through the dancing crowds with trays laden with at least 40 beers and 24 shots resting on top. Have a Jägerbomb or two and beam back at the sea of smiling faces welcoming you. The authentic Austrian après-ski experience has begun – let the good times roll.

03 / PARTY IN YOUR SKI BOOTS

Step out from the Pic Blanc cable car above Alpe d'Huez and the giant peaks of the Alps greet you. Standing at 3,300m, the view takes in the majestic La Meije, the Ecrins National Park and, in the far distance, Mont Blanc, no doubt slumbering beneath a beret of cloud.

But focus on the immediate view and Sarenne, the world's longest black run, winds down beneath you, all 16km of it. It's waiting to be carved up and explored, through a remote glacial valley far, far away from the masses cruising the rest of Alpe d'Huez.

While it is a run of two halves, strong intermediates shouldn't have any difficulty on it. The top half is narrow and challenging with stunning views and the bottom shallows out and meanders through the Gorges de Sarenne.

Tackle it just before lunchtime and you'll have worked up enough of an appetite to enjoy a tasty tartiflette on the terrace of the Auberge de la Combe Haute. At the end of the run, it's the perfect spot to toast your achievement.

04 / ALL BLACK AND WHITE

The early bird catches the worm and the early-rising skier gets the best turns. So first thing in the morning, board the helicopter to one of the blockbuster descents surrounding the resorts of Courmayeur, Cervinia, La Thuile or Monterosa, and clip in for up to 1,500 metres of untouched, untracked powder with just you, your guide and three others to share it with.

Surely there must be a catch? Nope. Aosta Valley is the home of affordable heli-skiing adventures and whilst an experience like this can sometimes cost upwards of the price of a small car, in Aosta Valley, you can have a one-day taster as part of an unforgettable long weekend for not much more than the price of a lift pass. And after a day of such extravagant action, there's no better place to relive the action than in the lounge of the luxurious St Hubertus Hotel in Cervinia or Pilier d' Angle in Courmayeur. You've earned it.

05
NOT JUST FOR HIGH FLIERS

MY FAIR LADY
06 \

You haven't experienced luxury until you've experienced Fairmont luxury, and in this corner of Alberta, Canada, you'll find three of the group's most iconic properties.

Start with the majestic Fairmont Banff Springs hotel, styled on a Scottish Baronial castle and with grandeur to match its surrounding ski slopes. Since its construction in 1888, it has set new standards in hospitality and even welcomed royalty.

On the other side of the Banff National Park and also in a UNESCO World Heritage Site, sits the Fairmont Chateau Lake Louise in elegant repose beside the sparkling blue lake.

You should make this your next stop before completing your lap of luxury at the Fairmont Jasper Park Lodge, where the comfort is divine and the surrounding mountains and lakes are captivating.

SHAKEN, NOT STIRRED
007 \

If there's one man who epitomises living the dream more than any other, it's Bond. James Bond. And if you want to tap into his lifestyle, you need head no further than the charming village of Mürren, in the Bernese Alps, Switzerland.

From here, you can recreate his daring skiing role in 'On her Majesty's Secret Service'. Take the cable car up to the top of the Schilthorn and make a pit stop for a special Bond breakfast in Piz Gloria, the revolving restaurant at 2,970m that had a starring role in the film. The views are spectacular, with the trio of the Eiger, Mönch and Jungfrau immediately ahead and the 200 plus peaks of the rest of the Alps stretching out behind.

But don't stay for too long, there's Bond action to be getting on with and Blofeld may catch up with you. Dropping away beneath you is a long piste with 1,300m of vertical to descend; enough variety to keep you (and Bond) entertained.

You may want to stop once or twice to soak up the glorious views but the most pressing thing is to get to the bottom unscathed. Seeing as you're recreating a key James Bond moment from film history, your chances should be high.

Lake Tahoe is a spectacular destination. Set in the heights of the Sierra Nevada Mountains, 22 miles of deep blue water stretches from north shore to south. Nestled among those mountains are 14 varied and enticing ski resorts waiting to welcome you. Straddling the California / Nevada border, some of the best skiing in the United States can be found around this beautifully blue piece of water, and what better way could there be to spend a fortnight than by touring them all? This is the ultimate destination for your California ski safari!

Start at the southern end of the lake with Heavenly, one of Tahoe's biggest and highest resorts. By day, explore the mainly wooded slopes with breathtaking views of the lake; by night take in the lively entertainment. While you're down south, check out Sierra-at-Tahoe and Kirkwood too, before heading round to the north shore and continuing your epic adventure. Check out Squaw Valley, home of the 1960 Winter Olympics, Northstar-at-Tahoe and nine more amazing resorts. Soak up the views of the lake, the snow-capped peaks and the California sun. With such outstanding scenery, it's a good job the skiing's first class too.

08 \
CALIFORNIA DREAMING

AWAY
09 \

The thwack of the ball against the polo mallet accompanied by the pounding of horses' hooves has historically been only accessible to the rich and privileged, but head to Klosters in January and not only can you watch the exhilarating Berenberg Snow Polo tournament for free, it's set against the backdrop of the 300km of pistes running across the Davos Klosters mountains.

Set in the pretty Alpine village loved by Royals and skiers alike, next to Davos, Europe's highest town, snow polo in Klosters is open to everyone and played in the evening, so after a full day's skiing, watch a chukka or two and enjoy a glass of mulled wine with friends. The glistening snow, the sinewy horses, the moonlight – it makes for a magical experience.

PARK AND GLIDE 10

It's tough to tear yourself away from the slopes in Alberta, where dry fluffy snow falls in every resort. But travel the road between three of its leading resorts, Banff, Lake Louise and Jasper, and you'll be in for a whole host of new thrills.

Don't let the distance on Highway 93 put you off. This is no ordinary highway, this is known as the Icefields Parkway, and it cuts through some of the Canadian Rockies' most dramatic scenery. So settle back behind the wheel and let the open road unfold in front of you.

While you could do the whole drive in four hours, you'll more likely want to spend double at least – there are towering peaks, rugged lumbering glaciers and frozen waterfalls to gaze at and explore, and if you're lucky you could be spotting elk, big horn sheep and moose too.

Pack a lunch and a Thermos and soak up the picturesque spots near the stunning Athabasca Falls or Crowfoot Glacier, happy in the knowledge there is plenty of the Icefields Parkway yet to see, and a resort awaiting your arrival as equally epic as the one you left behind.

SKI SUNDAY...
AND MONDAY,
TUESDAY,
WEDNESDAY...
11 \

Claim your place in racing history with a run down the Hahnenkamm, the most notorious fixture on the World Cup calendar. The racing circuit rolls into Kitzbühel in late January, so join in with the massive party, the cheering and cattle-bell ringing as the pros tackle this beast of a run.

Once it's over, it's your chance to shine as the downhill course opens up to the public. Known as the Streif (the stripe), the 3.3km course tears down the Hahnenkamm peak, at gradients of up to 85° and over lips that can send you up to 80 metres through the air, before ending in a huge mogul field in full view of the resort. The racers reach speeds of up to 90mph on it – only the brave need apply.

Japan is a land of many astounding sights, but none more so than the Japanese macaques, or snow monkeys, enjoying themselves in onsen, the naturally hot springs found across the volcanic islands of Japan.

Have your camera ready to capture them – as one of the most intelligent species on the planet, their expressive red faces and human behaviour, such as rolling balls of snow for fun and bathing in the pools, are images you'll want to save forever.

And the pools are open to the public to take a dip in too – surrounded by the fluffy powder snow that Japan is renowned for, the water is soothingly warm and the steam cocoons you. And if you're lucky, the snow monkeys may just clamber into the pool for a soak too…

12 /
MONKEY BUSINESS

IT MUST BE LOVE
13 \

In a resort the size of Aspen, it's easy to get away from it all and find some space for just the two of you. Skiers and snowboarders are spread across four mountains and 5,305 acres, so if it's a love-ski you're after, it'll feel like you've got the place to yourselves.

Whether it's romance you seek or just an aphrodisiac for life, enjoy a day on the slopes, gliding through the trees or cruising the groomers. Why not unwind in one of the spas, tuck or into a glamorous five-star dinner in town and then round the Aspen experience off by relaxing in front of a log fire. We're confident you'll fall in love with Aspen in no time.

For a foodie experience to send you to seventh heaven, look no further than Courmayeur in Italy's Aosta Valley. There must be something in the water of this small town, as a plethora of delicious, local produce and gourmet restaurants fill the place.

After a morning skiing the tree-lined slopes, either a pizza at the rustic and welcoming Rifugio Maison Vielle or a refined pasta dish at the smart Chiecco make a satisfying lunch.

But save some space for later – dinner's a big occasion here. Both the famous Fontina cheese and the mountain-herb cured Jambon des Bosses are protected 'designation of origin' products from the area so the resort's restaurants are full of gourmet treats.

Meat lovers should try Al Camin, while the wine list at Aria is not to be missed. Good job there's skiing to burn it all off!

14 /
BUON
APPETITO

If it's thigh-deep powder turns you seek, book yourself on the next flight to British Columbia's Kicking Horse and don't forget to pack your snorkel. Not only does this Canadian resort have an impeccable record for fresh snow, it's just 60 minutes away from the comfortable base lodge of the Great Canadian Heli-Ski Company (GCHS), the gateway to the powder-choked Selkirk and Purcell mountains.

With helicopter access to 110,000 acres of exclusive terrain, and groups limited to four people plus a guide, the opportunities for face shots full of powder are endless.

Wide open bowls and valleys spread out before you to carve up in huge arcs while narrow tight couloirs offer more technical challenges, above or below the treeline, and all to the breathtaking backdrop of the Canadian Rockies.

GCHS offers unlimited vertical so the only thing holding you back is your own ability—use the nearby slopes of Kicking Horse wisely and get in some powder practice. This is an opportunity too good to miss out on.

15 \ DON'T FORGET YOUR SNORKEL

LA FOLIE, C'EST JOLIE

If there's one place you should stop for refreshments on the slopes above Val d'Isère, it's the Folie Douce. It may look like any other mountain restaurant, albeit a smart one, but linger into the afternoon and BOOM, the party starts and the huge terrace comes alive with music, dancing and many smiley, happy people.

Entertaining the crowd with a unique mix of house music and live musical accompaniment are several singers, a saxophonist and a DJ, led by the exuberant Kely Starlight. As the beats warm the crowd up, the band mingle among the dancing throng, leap up onto the bar and can even be spotted on the roof, doing whatever it takes to entertain the international crowd.

Come snow or shine, champagne flows; particularly in the VIP area where, if you click your fingers, a bottle arrives by mini cable car straight from the bar. Dance anywhere near Kely and you'll no doubt be covered in a spray of bubbles many times throughout the afternoon – it's one of his favourite tricks for the up for it crowd. The party crescendos to a climax at 5pm but don't despair, return tomorrow and the Folie will be in full swing, ready to welcome you with open arms again.

DESCENTE ←

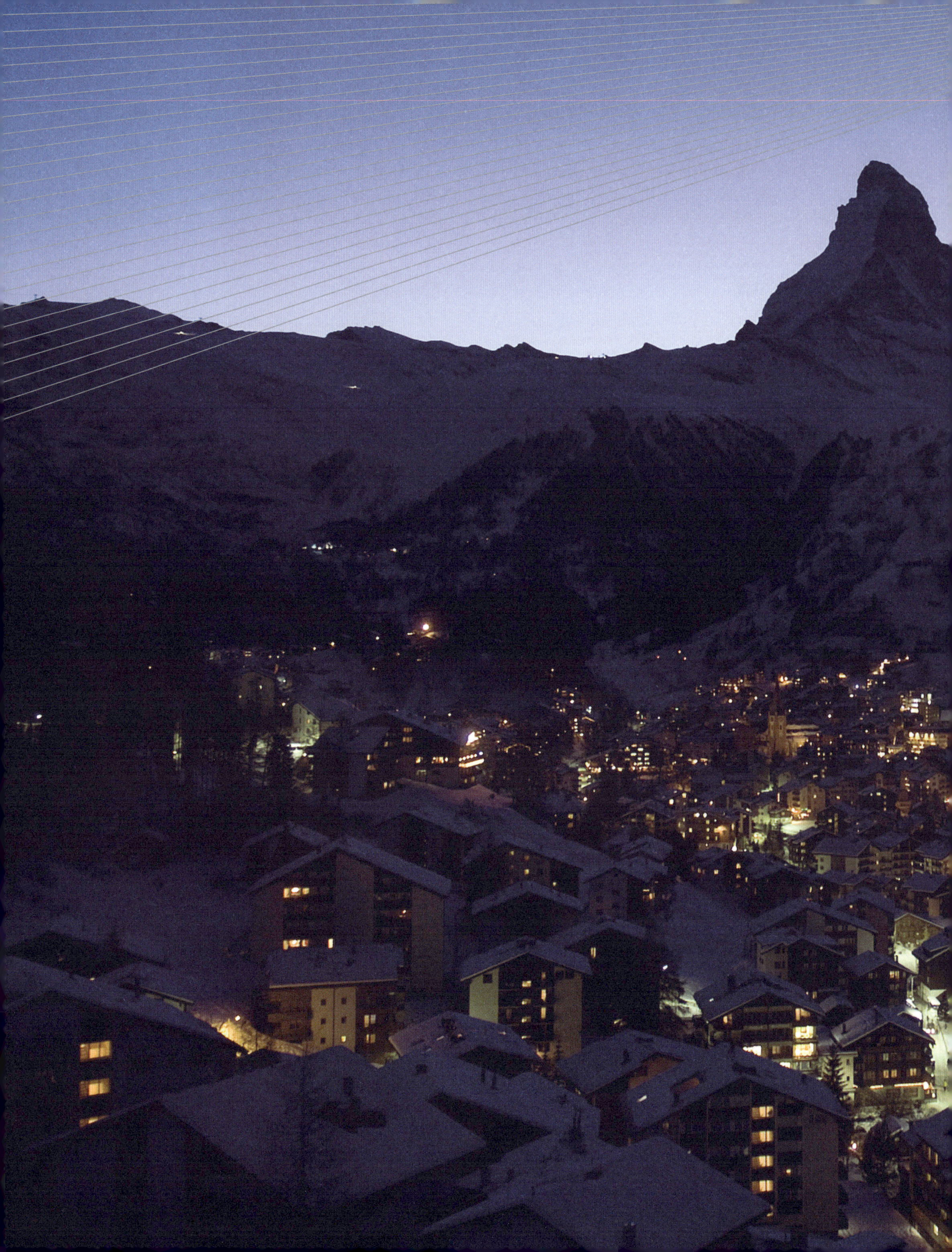

Visit Zermatt and you can't help but be awed by the presence of the Matterhorn. The stark, angular peak that soars up into the sky presides over Zermatt like a benevolent God, creating majesty and mystery in equal measure.

It's an inspirational mountain so it's of no great surprise that you'll find some of the finest dining in the Alps in this small town and on the slopes surrounding it. You'll want to stay longer than a week however – over 100 restaurants bask in the Matterhorn's glory, serving everything from seven-course gastronomic feasts in a restaurant like Zum See, to simple, local specialities of fondue and rösti.

Pick a restaurant with a view of the Toblerone summit, and tuck in – there's no need to be too fussy about which one. In the shadow of the Matterhorn you're certain to be dining in style.

17 \ VIEW FROM THE TOP TABLE

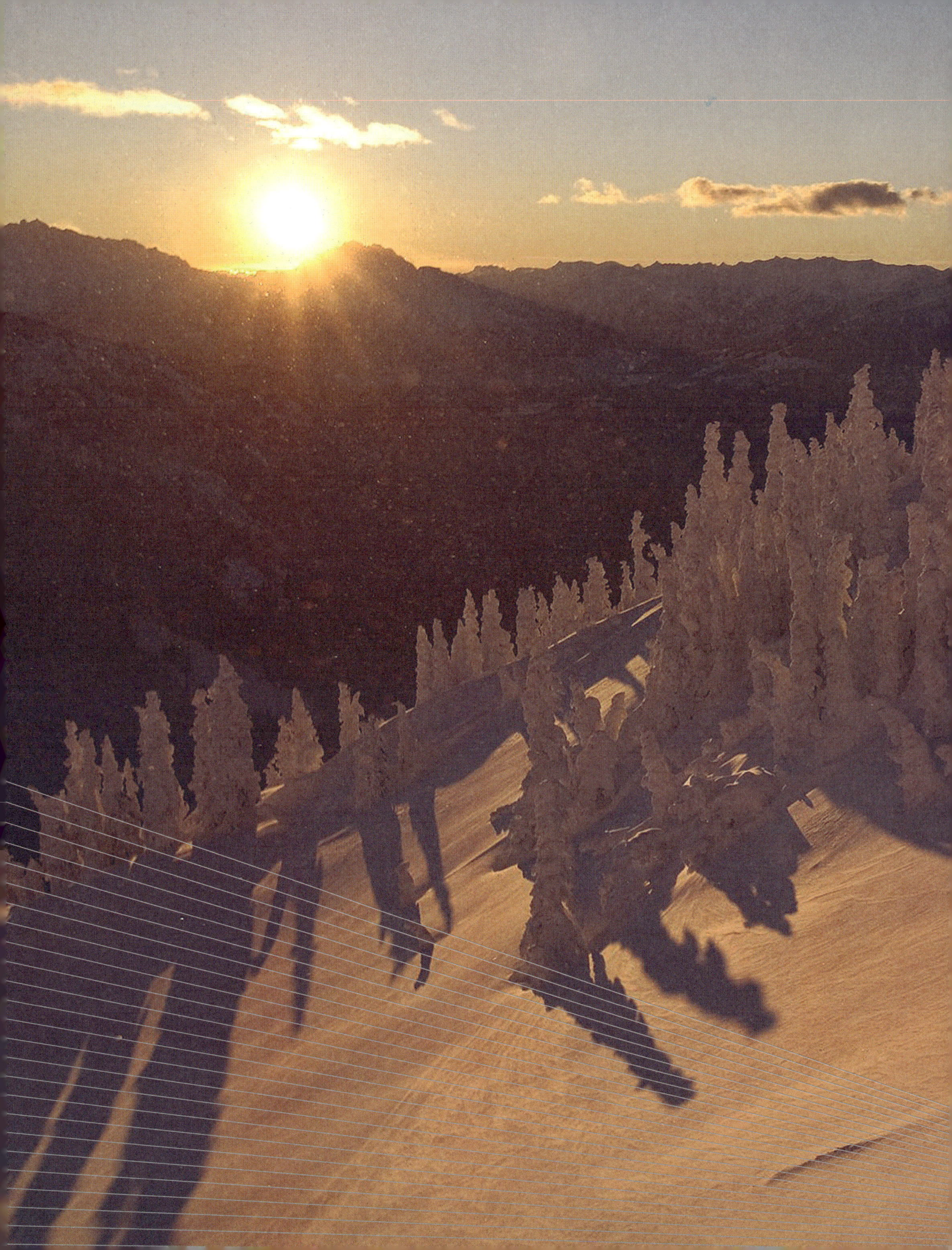

PEAK TO CREEK
18 /

In Whistler Blackcomb, British Columbia, the most iconic of resorts in Canada's snow-drenched Coastal Mountains, experience the absolute best of what's on offer with a day on both peaks.

Spend the morning skiing the wooded slopes and glades on Blackcomb Mountain before crossing to Whistler Mountain on the unique PEAK 2 PEAK Gondola.

Spanning 4.4km to join the two mountains and with glass-bottomed cabins, you're guaranteed a birds-eye view of the 8,000-plus acres of terrain spread out at your ski tips just waiting to be explored.

Refuel on the sunny terrace at Steeps Grill before tackling Whistler Mountain's slopes. But save some energy for the dramatic home run; Peak to Creek – all 1,500 vertical metres of it. Back at the base, congratulate yourself with a beer on the patio at Dusty's Bar and BBQ – you've just experienced a day of awesome proportions.

LAAX

For a cutting edge holiday, pay a visit to the Brits, the British Snowboard and Freeski Championships and week-long après-ski party in March. It's a showcase of all that's new and fresh in the snowsports scene, so it's fitting that it's held in LAAX, Switzerland, home to some of the most forward-thinking, award-winning architecture on the planet. With the striking rough-hewn stone and glass rocksresort and signinahotel, as well as the groundbreaking Riders Palace, LAAX is as stylish off the slopes as it is on. And with 220km of pistes, four terrain parks, Europe's largest halfpipe and first indoor freestyle hall, whether you're a competitor, spectator or partygoer, you couldn't be catered for better.

19 \
PARK LIFE

THE WILD, WILD WEST

Reach new frontiers on your next skiing holiday with a trip to Telluride, the original Wild West town in the San Juan Mountains in Southwest Colorado. While saloon bars and turn-of-the-century buildings line the beautiful old mining town streets and the ghost of Butch Cassidy lingers in the breeze, up above is some world-class terrain that is pushing new boundaries of its own.

Palmyra Peak and the Gold Hill Chutes are recent additions to the 2,000 acres of steep and deep slopes, and for immediate access to these challenging slopes and the plentiful more benign blues, stay at the smart Mountain Village, the alpine-inspired resort on the snow. But for the authentic cowboy experience, you'd better stay in Telluride, linked to Mountain Village by a free gondola. Either way, saddle up – you're in for a treat in Telluride.

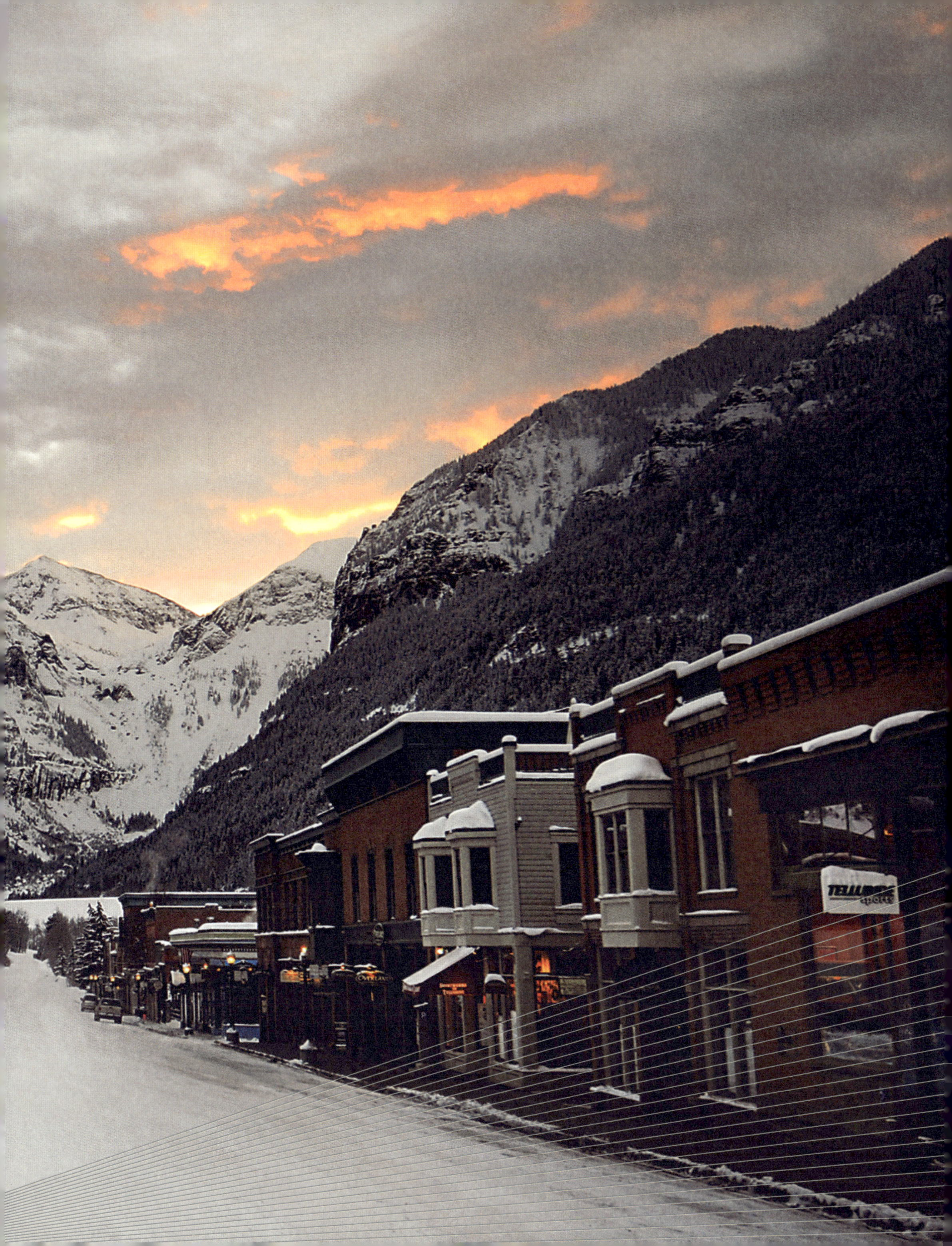

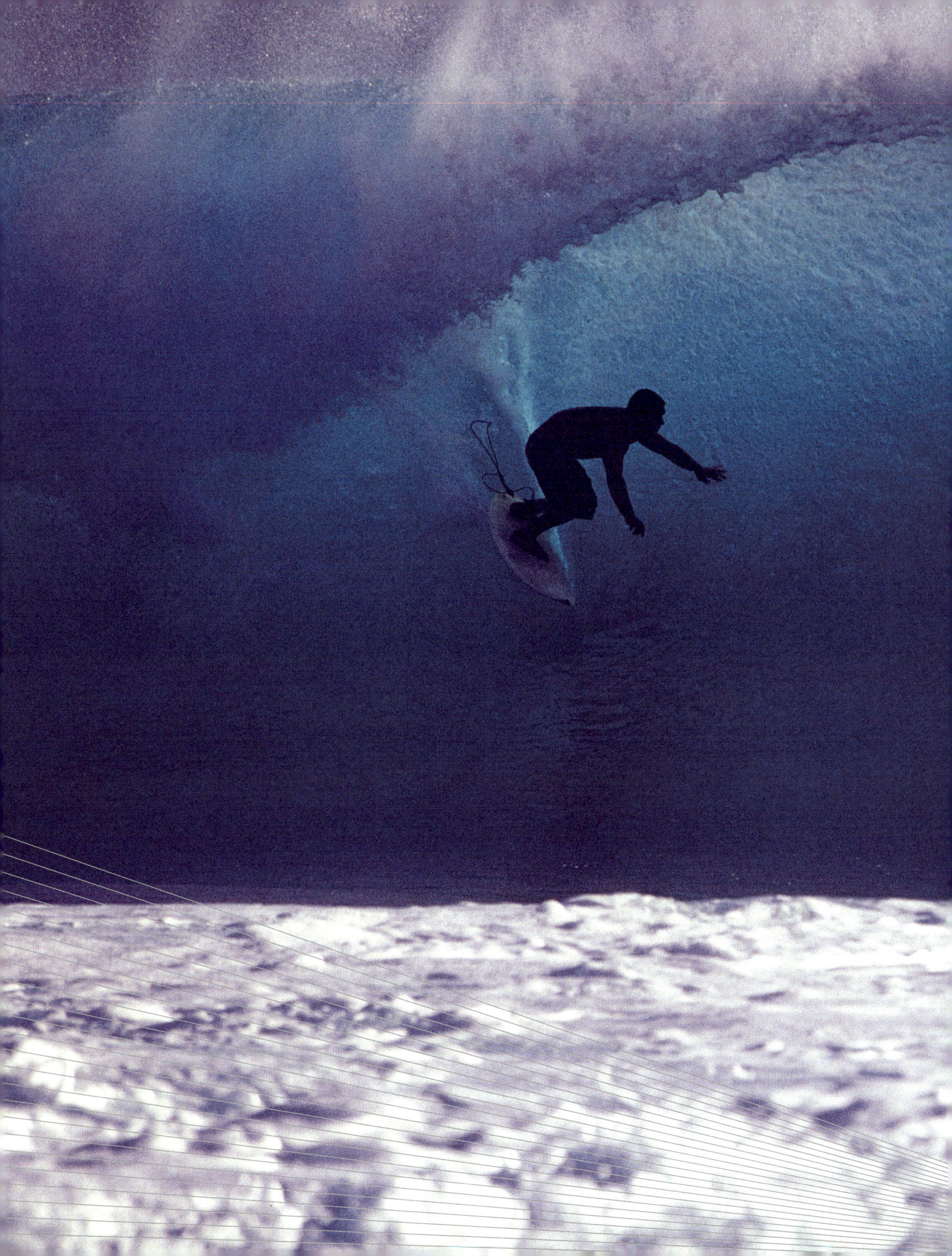

SUN, SKI, SURF
21 /

Combine the best of your winter and summer worlds with a ski and sun combination to Whistler and Hawaii. Spend a week in Whistler, riding the white stuff, cruising the groomers and tearing through the pow. Then deftly swerve the end of holiday blues by hopping across the Pacific to nearby Hawaii, where you can continue to ride the white stuff – only here it's of the more liquid variety.

Ride the waves of Honolulu beach or just soak up the rays and relax after the exhilarating slopes and après of Whistler. Either way, you'll have enough tales to turn your friends green with envy on your return, and your winter and summer holidays will never be the same again.

A TOUCH OF CLASS
22

Heated chairlift seats, impeccable slope grooming and lobster for lunch – not the key attributes of your average ski resort. But then Lech is just that little bit more luxurious than the norm. This beautiful, exclusive village in Austria's snow-sure Arlberg region is the playground of the rich and famous, but welcomes anyone who wants to ski like a lord or lady for the week. Sumptuous 4-star and 5-star hotels line the main street with plenty of opportunities for an indulgent lunch or an evening aperitif.

If you can tear yourself away from the luxury of your hotel, you might want to ski the White Ring, a 22km circuit covering 5,500m of altitude from Lech to neighbouring Zürs, and back again. If you're not feeling quite so energetic you could take a ride in a horse-drawn sleigh or simply sip a cocktail on one of the hotels' heated terraces and watch the world go by. Everyone deserves a touch of luxury.

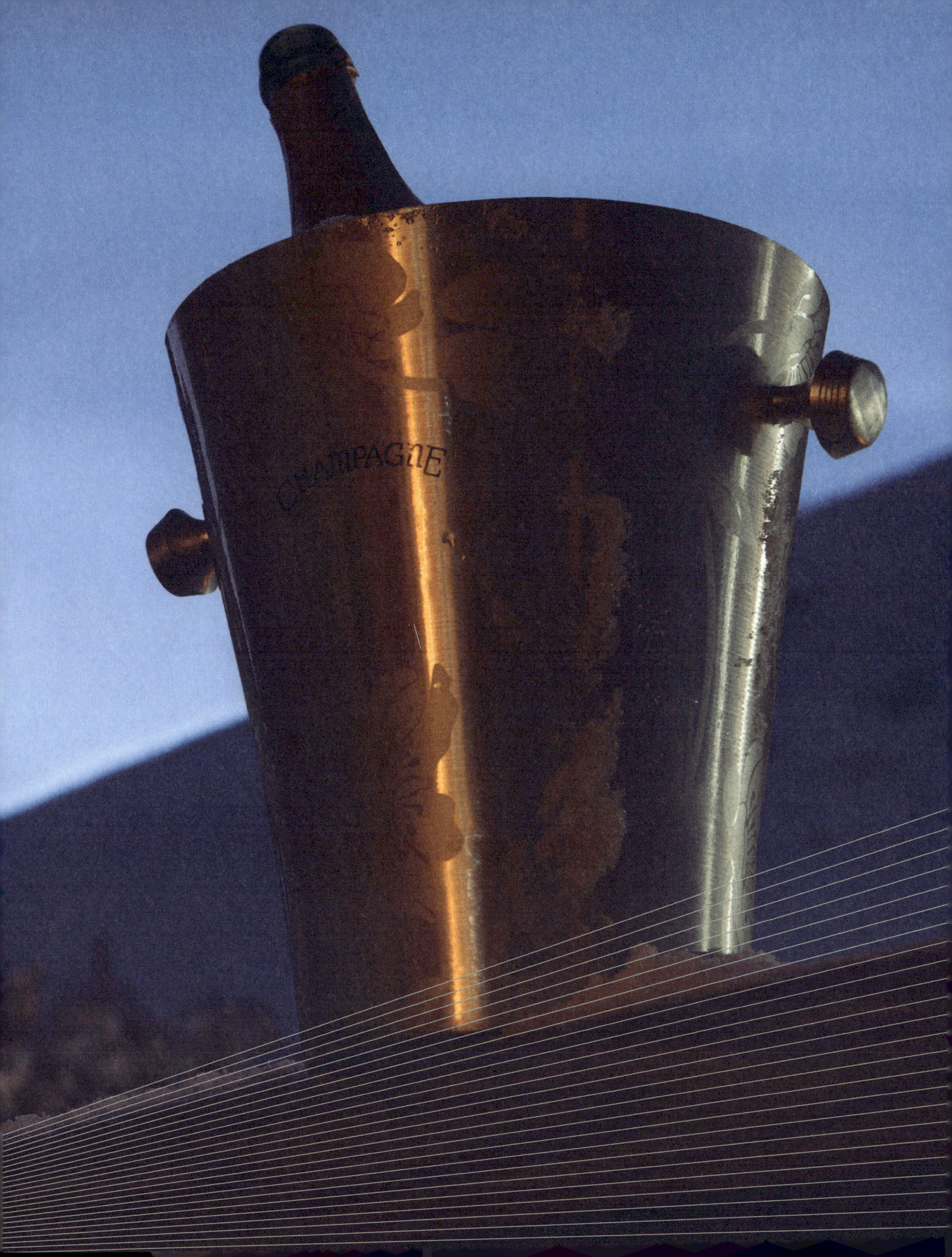
CHAMPAGNE

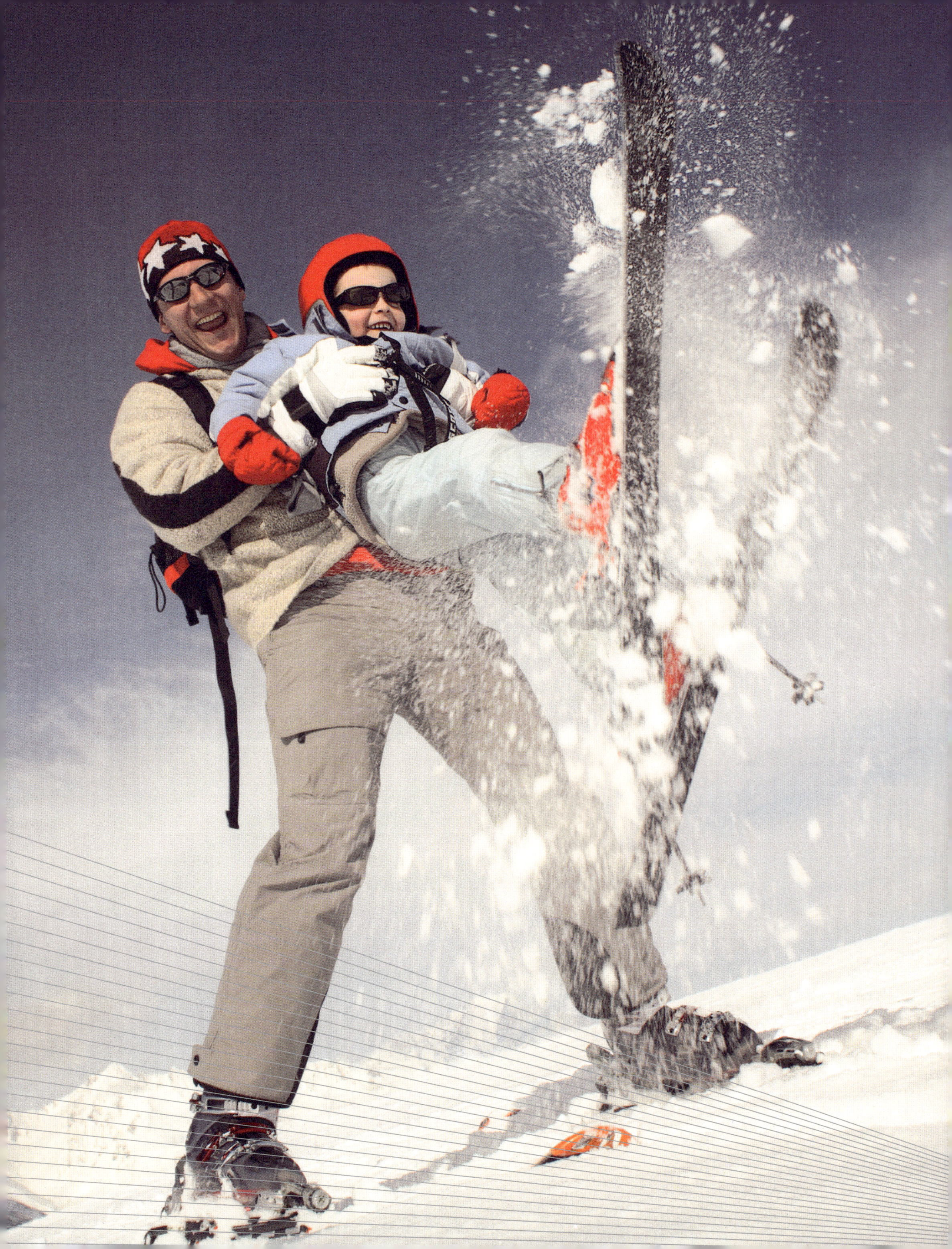

IT'S A FAMILY AFFAIR
23

Treat the family to the authentic Swiss skiing experience with a holiday to Saas Fee. The original chocolate-box village oozes alpine charm with its traditional wooden chalets and church spires, surrounded by 4,000m peaks and glaciers. As a welcoming and family-friendly place to let the kids really enjoy themselves, it can't be beaten. The traffic-free streets are safe to wander and the gentle, sunny nursery slopes are perfect for making those first tentative tracks on.

If they outgrow the beginners' area, there are 100km of slopes to explore and, for something a little different, there's a whole separate mountain to play on that's dedicated to tobogganing. When enjoyed under moonlight, it's a real adventure and the whole holiday will keep your kids smiling for weeks after.

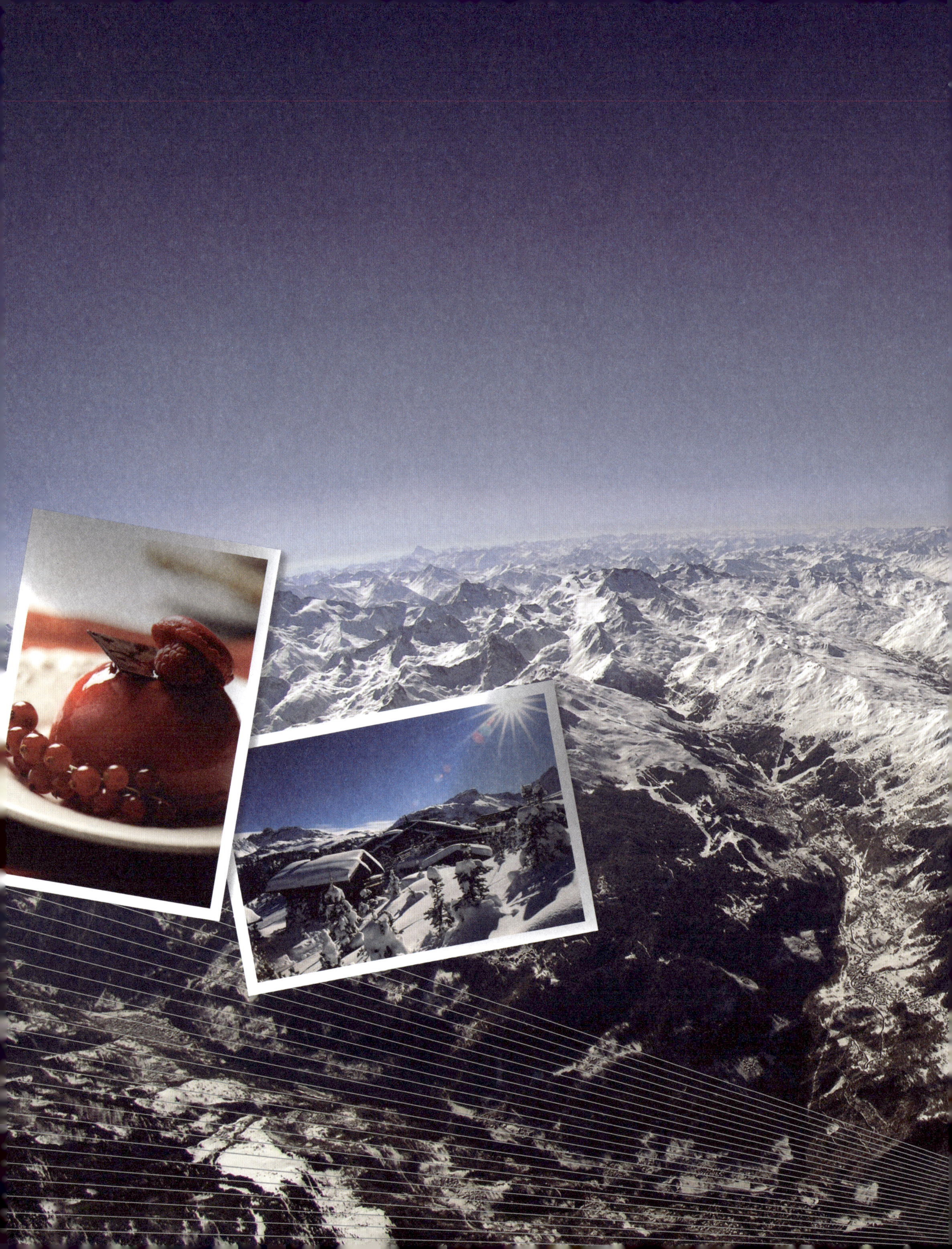

SKI TO
THE STARS
24 /

When a ski region's Michelin-starred restaurants are as twinkly and numerous as the stars in the night sky above it, you know you're onto a good thing. And that's just the case in the 3 Vallées where delicious, gourmet Michelin-rated restaurants fill not only the villages, but are scattered across the slopes too. For a week's skiing like no other, why not try a different one each day?

Start the week in Val Thorens at L'Oxlays, home to the youngest Michelin-starred chef of his time and it's also the highest Michelin-starred restaurant in Europe at 2,300m. Next, descend to 1,350m and into La Tania where you'll find Le Farçon and uncomplicated gastronomy. Spanning the altitudes between, don't miss the amazing father and son team at La Bouitte in St Martin de Belleville, and Le Bateau Ivre and Le Chabichou both in Courchevel 1850. Here's a tip - make sure you get a good ski under your belt in the morning, as after you've lunched at these places, all you'll be capable of is a leisurely run home. Ahh, delicious.

Over the years, we've enjoyed making holiday dreams come true for over 200,000 people, and to celebrate our 25th birthday, we don't want to receive presents, we want to give them – presents of dreams come true for kids who might not even see their next birthday.

So we've teamed up with Make-A-Wish Foundation® UK, which creates experiences of a lifetime for children and young people with life-threatening illnesses.

CHALLENGE OF A LIFETIME
25 \

Our goal is to raise £250,000 for Make-A-Wish Foundation® UK and every holiday we book for you will get us closer to that goal for them. That's not all though – we've a bunch of ways we're raising money and having fun doing it along the way, and we'd love you to share in this.

One fun way you can participate is to join us on our Ski the World Challenge Event in the Alps and ski the combined height of the World's tallest peaks across its seven continents – 43,314m in all.

Find out more and see which celebrities are joining in at www.skisolutions.com/makeawish and, together, we'll make their dreams a reality.

If you would like to find out more about
any of the experiences in this book,
visit **www.skisolutions.com/experience**

SKI
SOLUTIONS

UNPARALLELED SINCE 1986